D0582245

Published 2015 by Geddes & Grosset, an imprint of The Gresham
Publishing Company Ltd, Academy Park, Building 4000,
Gower Street, Glasgow, G51 1PR, Scotland

Copyright © 1996 The Gresham Publishing Company Ltd
Endpaper images copyright © Attitude, courtesy of Shutterstock

All rights reserved. No part of this publication may be reproduced,
stored in a retrieval system or transmitted in any form or by
any means, electronic, mechanical, photocopying, recording or
otherwise, without the prior permission of the copyright holder.

Conditions of Sale:
This book is sold with the condition that it will not, by way of trade
or otherwise, be resold, hired out, lent, or otherwise distributed or
circulated in any form or style of binding or cover other than that
in which it is published and without the same conditions being
imposed on the subsequent purchaser.

ISBN 978-1-910680-61-2

Printed and bound in Malaysia

9 10

ABC

Judy Hamilton
Illustrated by Beverley Sprio

Tarantula
EARLY LEARNERS

Aa

Apple

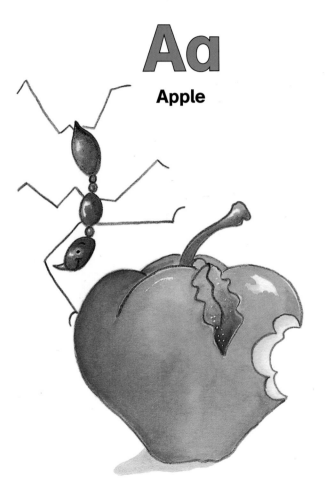

Aah! There's **an a**nt on my **apple**!
He's quite **an a**crobat!

Bb

Bear

Belinda the **bear b**ounces **b**y with her **b**ig **b**lue **b**all.

Cc
Cat

Clara the **cat** eats **c**arrots to **c**ure herself of her **c**old and **c**ough.

Dd
Dog

Douglas the **dog d**ozes in the **d**oorway, **d**reaming of his **d**inner.

Ee
Elephant

Ernest the **elephant** gets his **e**xercise **e**very day, juggling **e**ggs.

Ff
Fish

Fish can't play **f**ootball.
Fish have **f**ins, not **f**eet!
Not **f**air!

Gg

Goat

Gus the **goat** plays in **g**oal on the **g**reen.
Go, **G**us, **g**o!

Hh

House

Hattie's **house** is **h**alfway up the **h**ill.
Hattie's **h**ouse is **h**uge!

Ink

Indian **ink** is **i**mpossible to wash out.
Invisible **ink** is **i**mpossible to see.

Jj

Jack-in-the-box

James has **j**ust bought a **jack-in-the-box** at the **j**umble sale. **J**ust look at it **j**ump!

Kk
Kite

King **K**evin is flying his **kite**.
Keep it up, **K**evin!

Ll
Lion

Leonard the **lion** lounges in the long grass after lunch. Leonard sleeps like a log!

Mm
Mouse

Mary the **mouse** found a **m**uffin.
"**M**m! **M**arvellous!" she **m**umbled
as she **m**unched.

Nn
Nurse

Nancy the **nurse** works at **n**ight.
Nancy is **n**ifty with a **n**eedle!

Octopus

Oliver is no **o**rdinary **octopus**.
Oliver is **o**range!

Pp
Penguin

Percy **Penguin p**osed by the **p**ool
in **p**urple **p**yjamas.

Qq
Queen

The **queen** felt **q**ueasy as she waited in the **q**ueue. **Q**uite **q**uietly, she left.

Rr

Rabbit

Robert **Rabbit r**an **r**ather well in the **r**ace.
But **R**achel **r**ushed past him and won.

Ss
Seaside

Sausages get **s**lightly **s**andy if you **s**izzle them at the **seaside**!

Tt
Tiger

Tigers can get **t**erribly **t**etchy if you **t**read
on **t**heir **t**oes!

Uu Umbrella

Uh-oh! Rain!
Up with your **umbrella**!

Vv Violin

Vincent plays the **violin**
in his **v**est.

Ww
Winter

Wear your **w**oollies to keep yourself **w**arm!
Winter can be **w**indy and **w**et!

Xx X-ray

Look at your bones in an **X-ray**!
Look for **x** in words like fo**x** and bo**x**.

Yy Yacht

Have **y**ou seen a **y**ellow **yacht** like this one?

Zz
Zebra

Zebedee looked after the **zebras** in the **z**oo.
Zebedee wore a jacket with a **z**ip.